A Raw Business Sense

"How I went from $8hr to $15,000 a Month"

By
Lamont Troy Taylor, Sr.

Copyright 2010 by Lamont Troy Taylor, Sr.
All rights reserved
Including the right of reproduction
In whole or in part in any form
Published by Taylor and Taylor Publishing House

Taylor and Taylor Publishing House
P.O. Box 1952
Easton, Maryland 21601

Manufactured in the United States of America

Library of Congress Cataloging in Publication Data

Taylor, Lamont T., Sr.
A Raw Business Sense "How I went from $8 to $15K a Month"

ISBN -10: 0615356443
ISBN -13: 9780615356440

This book is dedicated in memory of my loving mother the

Late Gwendolyn Catherine Taylor, without her, I would not have developed the raw talent, this book is also dedicated to my beautiful wife Rachel who has been supportive of me in my many business ventures, even when opportunities seemed nonexistent. To my future raw entrepreneurs- Pierce, Keirien, Emily, and Lamont Jr., for this book are written as a guide and I pray that you may find it useful in business and in life.

Aside from family, this book is written specifically for all the people that are business minded,

People that want to have a better life,

Those that want to change their life,

Those that want to get into business, but are not sure of it.

Especially for the people who do not believe that they have what it takes

Those who do not believe that they are smart enough, and

For those that believe that they are financially challenged.

For all of you…this book is a must.

-*Lamont Troy Taylor, Sr.*

Table of Contents

Introduction 1
In the Beginning 5
How to Change Your Mindset 11
How to Put Forces in Motion 13
Give a Helping Hand 21
The Raw Turning Point 23
Lamont's 40 Rules to Raw Business Success 45
Lamont's Raw Business Policies 67
Making Good Financial Decisions 84
Re-investing Back Into the Business 85
Keeping Some Liquid 85
It's Not Your Account…It's the Businesses' Account 86
Where the Raw Business Investment Comes From 86
A Grass Root Raw Business Man 87
See a Physician 87
How to Obtain Coverage 87
Preventative Maintenance 88
Offsetting Stress and Illnesses 88
Maintain a Balance 89
Your Intake is Your Fuel 89
Reach out to the World 89

"KNOW THAT YOU CAN DO ANYTHING YOU WANT."

-Lamont Troy Taylor, Sr.

Introduction

When thinking about writing this book, I tried to imagine someone going to the bookstore and picking my book off of the shelf and looking at it, which is why I do not believe that it is by chance that you are reading this book. The mere fact that you have chosen this book means that you have set forces in motion to bring you the information that you desire. Whether the reason for you selecting the book is for success, wealth, happiness, or motivation, you will find the answers that you are looking for within these pages.

From this point on disregard all preconceived perceptions as to what makes one a success. Pump yourself up! You already are a success RIGHT NOW! This book will fine tune your skills and mind-set to launch you to achieving your deepest desires.

Have you ever seen others living the life that you only dream of? Are you tired of reading books that identify a problem, but they do not offer a step by step solution to change these problems. Well look no further, I am going into great detail on how a high school dropout working a part time job went from making $8 per hour to over

$15,000 a month with no experience or knowledge in the industry that I built my business.

I want to inspire you. I want you to have access to the information that can get you the things that you want out of life. I want you to be able to succeed in your business goals, obtain your health goals, and achieve your financial freedom. This book includes all of the things that I wish I could have picked up and read in a book, while I was experiencing things in life trying to get ahead.

Starting my own business never crossed my mind. My mindset was to just get a job. That is all I knew. That is all my parents new. That is all that their parents knew, so I just adopted that way of thinking. Although I was never comfortable working a job for others. I just never seemed to agree with the process. I did it, but it is just that some internal mechanism within me will not allow me to agree with it. I cannot put my finger on it, but working for others just did not work for me. The advantages and disadvantages of working for others for me is that I knew at the end of every week or every two weeks depending on the pay cycle of whatever job I was on, I knew that if I just showed up I would get paid. I began to form my living standards around the check so it became a form of security. I knew I could expect it. However, when my hours were cut, my standard of living that was based around that check was interrupted and it forced me into a mode of insecurity which caused me to look at other options. I needed money right away and I knew the only way that I could do that was to provide a service or to sell a product because at the end of that exchange, I could get paid. So, I decided to start my own business based on the need to maintain my lifestyle. Although actually I really did not have a lifestyle on that salary it was more or less my security.

> "START TODAY NOT TOMORROW, FOR YOU WILL BE ONE DAY CLOSER TO YOUR GOALS."
>
> -*Lamont Troy Taylor, Sr.*

In the Beginning

I was the type of kid that always liked to go and do something whether it was good or bad. I never wanted to sit in the house. For that reason, the one thing that I never had an issue with today or as a child is that I could and still can easily make friends. The ability to make friends easily transferred over when I started doing business. For example, I found it very easy to knock on doors and to talk to people. I was use to people being receptive to me and I accredit it to just "being myself" and being genuine as well as being upfront and honest with people as much as possible. My advice is that you need to maintain friendships and the ability to make friends no matter what stage you are in your business. Personal contact and the ability to socialize are both keys to success.

Growing up, I was very active in sports as well. You name it! I probably played every sport that there is that one can play. I was raised as the only child so I did not have any brothers or sisters to play with at home and things like that. That was why I was always out trying to find and play with different friends. While playing sports, I considered myself to be on a scale from 1 to 100 maybe 50% competitive and 50% just being a part of a team. I knew the object of the game was to win, but it was not my sole purpose in being a part of the sport. I enjoyed the teamwork. Today in business, I like to be competitive because I have to be. Because of the market today in business you have to have a competitive edge just to maintain in business. However, I still enjoy the team work and the efforts that my colleagues and I put together in getting out our products and services. In fact, I have found that working as a team can prove to be essential to developing a good product. Developing a good business team is crucial for developing the success of your business. You want to recruit team players who have the same goals as your team. You want to position your players in an environment in which they can be most productive for your company. For example, if someone has a background in marketing, you should not have them do your accounting. You want to be able to put them where their skills are required and learn to identify their strong points. A raw business person may not have a recruitment representative so he or she has to work to identify the skills and make placements accordingly.

Both of my parents are deceased and I was born in Cambridge, Maryland although, I spent the first part of my childhood growing up in Oxford, Maryland. I was raised by my mother and grandparents. My father passed away when I was very young, so I never got to see him or really meet him. Dr. Nelson Cleves Preyer was his name and I have been told that he was actually the first black dentist in Easton, MD. On the other hand, my mother mainly did house cleaning in Oxford, which is a fairly wealthy area. My grandma did the same type of work for a lot of wealthy folks. My grandfather worked at the local boat yard. Some of the work that my mother received was from my grandmother. As my grandmother aged she passed some of the work to my mom. If you think about it, back then a lot of time the mindset was more about getting a job. It was not focused on self employment. This too was my mindset prior to becoming a raw business man.

Naturally, I also shared a mindset on education at the time. My mother graduated and completed high school, my grandmother went as high as fifth grade and I am not certain if my grandfather ever went to school, which is probably why education was not that important to me at that time. Other than completing grades 1-12 and getting good grades, education was not stressed in our household. In fact, I was one of those students that thought school was very boring. It never held my attention. I would often find myself in class daydreaming. It just did not interest me. I would just go there and my attention was not held. Obviously, with that type of attitude, I fell behind in my grades and my scenario was a typical one: I started getting behind and it became harder to catch up and before I knew it I was so far behind I could not even try to catch up because I let myself get so far behind. I found myself sitting in class trying to entertain myself because the classroom was not holding my attention, so I had to occupy myself so I normally ended up disrupting others. To me it was just trying to have some fun or entertain myself but it was not the time or place so therefore I became a distraction and I decided that when I was of legal age that it just was not the place for me. I remember telling my mother that I decided to quit and her response was "Well...you better get yourself a job." As you see my mother's mindset was "I am not going to be taking caring of you, so if you quit you have to get a job and support yourself." At the end of the day the way that she thought and her parents thought was that "you get out... you get a job... you support your family". The whole idea is that since you quit school, it means you start your journey earlier now. If I were to assume their way of thinking I would say that school was just an expected process and that was the only purpose it served. So the process was for me to go through grades 1-12, complete it, come out and get a job.

While my mother and grandmother worked for a lot of affluent folks I got a chance to see how the other side lived. I got a chance to get out and see how the other houses were and they were a lot different from mine and so was their lifestyles. I think then I realized that there was another side of the tracks. I did not know how to get there. I did not know why I wanted to be there. I just knew that there was something better about the way that others were living than the way that I was living. But I knew that at the time my parents did not know to instill in me the concept to start my own business or to become self-employed. They wanted me to learn to work hard and to get a job. My father was self-employed he had his own dental practice in

Easton and my mom use to work for him. So he was always self-employed from what my mom told me. Apparently, my father had done his stint in the military and had been a Lieutenant in the Army but that he never liked taking orders and wanted to be his own boss. He went back to school and then dental school to become a dentist. That is probably where I received the entrepreneurial spirit. I received the "know how" from my mom's family. The "know how" and the "raw talent" comes from my mom.

I would have to say that what I learned from my mother and grandmother was their biggest focus…behavior. They seemed to be more concerned with my behavior and placed less emphasis on my education other than the less typical public education that others receive. They really wanted good manners and good behavior. That is what they hammered into me as a child growing up. As a parent, I am a lot different. I still believe in the manners and the discipline however I also focus on education, instilling a different mindset into my children to think differently than I thought when I was their age. I tell them that they can be anything that they want to be. I tell them that if they want to get a job then do it. They just have to put their minds to it and achieve it. What I tell my children is that the real key to success is to change your mindset and the way you think. I tell them "by changing your mindset and for people who want to change their situation they have to change their thinking".

> "IN ORDER TO CHANGE YOUR MINDSET, YOU MUST BE WILLING TO OPEN YOUR MIND TO DIFFERENT CONCEPTS."
>
> -Lamont Troy Taylor, Sr.

How to Change Your Mindset

Something has to kick in for the mindset to change. The mindset will continue to remain the same unless there are (1) other desires, (2) a will to have a change, (3) and/or a dramatic event. This must take place to cause the mind to want to change. Once that takes place, then you need the tools to help you to get the things that you desire which will cause you to think differently. This is where you start to take in information about what you want to do or interests in the things that you desire. From there, you will start to move towards the things you desire or want to obtain. Your mindset will gradually change in the direction that you are learning to grow in.

In order to keep advancing on that path:

Avoid anything that does not line up with your desire. This can be people, activities, actions, the words you use, the way you dress, the food you eat, the places you frequent and most of all it will change your outlook on your life and business.

"FORCES ARE PUT INTO MOTION BY YOUR THINKING AND YOUR ACTIONS."

-*Lamont Troy Taylor, Sr.*

How to Put Forces in Motion

Step A
Evaluate the Company You Keep

Take a look around at the company you keep and see if their minds align in the direction that you are getting ready to embark on. If they are of like minds, they will prove to be very inspirational and motivational. If they are not, CUT THEM OFF. For example, although not as extreme, some doctors will cut off a toe in order to save a leg. Likely so, some acquaintances could prove to be gangrene in your toe. You have to amputate them because they can consume you totally. I am not literally saying cut them or hurt them, however you may need to part company such as long conversations of nothing, stop gossiping, stop emailing, and stop hanging out just to do unproductive things. Replace them with new acquaintances that take on the same goals and desires that you have. When you start doing that you will start finding yourself to come in contact with people of the same interests. Once you drop the negative influences some of the negative activity discontinues because you are not doing it with them anymore. Do not succumb to pressure from your peers. Have the courage to stand alone in your decisions regardless of what someone else thinks.

Step B
Want More

Your desire will grow when you learn to want and expect more. Decide that you are going to make it happen. You may not know how or where, but you know what not to do. When you want to better yourself, it is not that necessary to know how, but once you start to seek out what you want you find that things will begin to open up for you.

Step C
Decide to do it

Once you make the decision to do it, stick with it and watch things start to unfold for you.

Step D
Believe that YOU Can Do It

Your belief in what you are doing governs the forces that **instruct** the needed forces in motion. In Genesis 1:3 "God said let there be light and there was light." If I believe in this theory I have to assume that God dwelled in total darkness and that the universe was conceived in total darkness and then there was light. Out of the darkness the universe came. What I try to tell my children is the same thing. Everything we see in the light comes from a concept, a thought, a vision, a belief and then it turns into a physical light that we can see. Everything that we see developed in the darkness of some man or woman's mind. So the start is a result of changing your mind and then everything will come into the light.

Step E
The Pursuit of Something Greater than Us

I am still trying to pursue and understand. It is an ongoing and growing experience with my spirituality. I am constantly trying to understand the true nature of God's role in our lives. I just know that we have to have something that is bigger than ourselves. We need something that we can fall on when times are difficult. That higher spirituality or Being that is higher than us. We cannot just take burdens on ourselves it could be too much. I am not trying to convert your belief; I am just trying to get you to understand that there is something greater than us. The fact remains that we do exist and we come from somewhere somehow. The question is where and no one knows. Something higher than ourselves has placed us here. We want to make the best of what we are given. The cards that we are dealt in life are not permanent because the deal with that is that we can actually change the cards that we are dealt. This gets back to one's mindset because we control our own destiny with the way we act and think, so we can actually change the cards that we are dealt if we so chose. It relates to business in the manner that by putting your mind to whatever you want to do you can do it.

Step F
Just Do It...You are Destined for Good Things

No matter what the cards you have been dealt are. No matter what you're financial status is or your education is. If you want to start a business you must first envision it in your mind and eventually it will begin to manifest itself. Like I mentioned previously my parents really did not install into me an entrepreneurial mindset, so they basically installed in me the attributes they had and the attributes that their parents installed into them. This mindset trickles down into every generation. This just does not just have to do with business. It translates to eating habits. I ate whatever my mom put on the plate. Controlling what we eat has a big part to do with our mindset. I had to become more conscious of the foods that I was taking into my body and the affects that they were having on my body whether they were good or bad. Our belief system absolutely ties into our financial status and situations because we believe that a lot of the finances especially in certain ethnic communities are unattainable so we do not attempt to achieve financial heights of freedom. We do not even try. These systems and this is a system that can hinder people because we are praying and hoping for some pie in the sky or something that is going to fall into our laps from prayer. The Good Book says in James 2:17 "Even so faith, if it have not works, is dead in itself", so we must have the **faith**, but also we must apply the **work**. It is more than just praying and waiting. We have to also develop our mindset and then go out and put some physical works to our goals.

Step G
You Must Develop Self-Discipline

I was quiet in my early teens, but at the same time, I was kind of wild and prone to getting into a lot of trouble by partying with my friends and hanging out. I was a loose cannon type of guy partying and drinking and stuff like that. I had already had my oldest son and I remember thinking my dad had never married my mom and he already had children, so I remember thinking I would never be one of those guys who had a bunch of children by different women and not get married. I said the next time I am getting married. My second son came and I stopped hanging out, stopped partying, and changed my friends. I just knew that I wanted to change my life, but at that particular moment I did not know what I wanted to do. I had dropped out of high school and I did not have any skills or trade. But I knew I wanted more and that there was more to life than what I was experiencing. So I began my quest for knowledge. I found myself the once "cool party animal" spending the majority of my time in bookstores. Barnes and Nobles became my new hang out. I also spent a lot of time at the Goodwill because I found that I could get college books that were turned in from college students for as little as $.25.

Step H
Search for Wisdom

At the height of my janitorial cleaning business when my financial status was fine and I felt very accomplished, I awoke on my sofa and I recall deciding that if I can do this great in business, that I could also go back and get my diploma. At this point, it was one of those things that I had never done and it bothered me because I felt not so accomplished because it hung over my head like the bad tag for being a high school dropout.

After seeing my success in my business even though I thought I could never do it, it gave me the proof that I needed to cause me to know that I could do more. At one point I thought about never going back and tackling it, it became easy to just go back and do it just for the sake of doing it. After achieving that with ease, I started questioning myself about college. After I got my diploma I thought "Why can't I go to college?" so I went and enrolled into my local community college and that was easy. All of these things that I thought were hard because I had created my own mental blocks had turned out to be fairly easy.

"DON'T FOCUS ON WHAT YOU CAN'T DO; FOCUS ON WHAT YOU CAN DO."

-Lamont Troy Taylor, Sr.

My first business was a reminder service that I saw on an infomercial. I was up late at night watching one of those infomercials and I thought to myself I am going to start my own business. The kitchen table was my desk. Man it was crazy! That pretty much got the ball rolling and I never turned back from entrepreneurship every since I got bit by that bug. Once you get bit by that bug and you realize that this is the direction you want to move in don't concern yourself with anything or anyone that you think may hinder you in the process. Do not worry about money. Do not worry about your experience. Do not worry about working at your kitchen table or having no office. Do not concern yourself with the lack of transportation. Don't be concerned with ways on how you can't do your business. Be concerned with ways on how you can start your business with the things that you do have.

Step I
It May Involve More than One Shot

Try different things. In some thought process it may have seemed as if I was aimless trying a bunch of different things. Trying things, but not sure what. If this happens, don't be discouraged. You have to find your way and what works for you. This may take several attempts. Each one of those experiences is a learning tool. Consider what you have learned from it. Take the experience and utilize it with your next business venture. Most of what I learned was from observation. If you figure, I never went to school or business school, so everything I learned was from observation and mimicking others in business. Just make sure that you mimic someone who is successful or has reached the level of success that you want. It does not hurt to ask people who are in the same industry. Stroke their ego. Say "I want to be like you" or "How did you get where you are?" You may be surprised how much people will answer if you ask them. They are always looking for the opportunity to lecture or teach. That way they are always giving back. I mentor anyone that I come in contact with that is interested in starting their business or just being a better person. In fact, if you would like for more direction or mentorship email me at ltaylor234@gmail.com .

> "UNDERSTAND THAT WHEN GIVING TO OTHERS, YOU ARE GIVING TO ONE'S SELF."
>
> *-Lamont Troy Taylor, Sr.*

Give a Helping Hand

My passion now is to continue to work for myself, provide for my family, and be an asset to my community and those that are around me. I also want to share with others and help them to accomplish their goals and dreams. I just feel that my life wouldn't be complete unless I was able to help somebody else achieve the success and happiness that I have been able to experience.

> "THINK, THINK, THINK
> AND THEN THINK
> SOME MORE."
>
> -Lamont Troy Taylor, Sr.

The Raw Turning Point

I do want to encourage people to think. This book should be an inspirational piece because I feel more and more people today are not inspired to do things that they are capable of doing. Most people think that it is very difficult to do these things. If you look at my janitorial business, I explain to people how I went from $8 an hour to over $15K per month. It started when my hours were cut and I was living in a two bedroom apartment with my wife and two children at the time. I was concerned about how I was going to take care of my family and I remember riding in my car thinking about how I was going to do this. I happened to notice houses that were really dirty and covered with pollen. A light bulb went off and I thought to myself, I think that those people would love to have their houses cleaned off and sprayed. So I decided to go buy a pressure washer for $130. I purchased one and made some flyers describing my new pressure washing business and I placed my cell phone number on the flyer. I just went out to those houses that seemed to have a need for pressure washing and I picked the dirtiest houses because I knew that those were the ones that I would have a better chance of landing. I pulled up to this house and I noticed it was in need of some pressure washing and without any appointment without any experience I just went up there and knocked on the guys door. It must have been around lunch time because I remember him coming to the door chewing a sandwich. I introduced myself and told him that I was in the area pressure washing the houses today and if he would be interested in getting a free quote. His reply was how much would it cost to pressure wash my house? At this point I knew he was considering me, so I knew I had to quote him a price that he would be compelled to take me up on the offer, it had to be such a deal that he could not afford to let it get away. Remember, I could not afford to have him question my experience or references because I had none so I had to cut him a price that would be a deal. And I charged him $35. He smiled and said when can you start? So I ended up pressure washing his whole house and his shed for $35. It took me approximately 2 hours. He was very satisfied and wrote me a check for $35 and I was off to the next house. So now with a reference I went to two or three houses down delivered the same spill and however this time I mentioned that I just did the residence down the road. Now my credibility had risen because I had done somebody else in the neighborhood. At this point I charged $55 for the house and I got the job. So that day I made $90 in about 4 hours, which is about $22.50 per hour. That was a big difference from the $8hr that I was use to getting and then had the rest of my day free. Since that day I have never looked back. I knew every since then I had to work for myself. It just took me being put under pressure and getting my hours cut to choose to do for myself. I have never been put in a position in which I had to do for my family and did not have any other alternatives. The next day I went out to Wal-Mart and I purchased one of those blue button-up service shirts because I wanted to have a more professional image. I went out and printed up more flyers and started taking them to buildings. I wanted to clean more commercial buildings and construction sites because I wanted to get involved with the post construction cleanup. Meanwhile I was still searching houses that needed to be pressured washed. I was averaging about 4 of those a week. So when I was not pressure washing I was passing out more flyers to get more work. Then I got a call from one of the post construction sites where I left one of my flyers on a pretty huge building and they needed someone to clean the windows. As I look back this job was probably too big for me at the time and I probably should have turned it down, but I thought I would figure it out and I accepted the job. So I began to clean the windows on the post construction site and I noticed the foreman kept looking at me and I know he thought "where are the rest of his guys" and I said to myself what I have to do is a good job and do it right and give them what they paid for they would overlook the fact that I am small and no employees. At the end of the day they would only look at the fact that they received a great job and a great price.

"INTERNAL BELIEF RADIATES ON THE OUTSIDE."

-Lamont Troy Taylor, Sr.

Then this is how things start to open up. As I was doing the job the owner of the building saw me in there cleaning up the post construction cleanup and he came up to me and said "we are going to need someone to continually clean up this building when it is done to maintain it". At this particular time I really did not have much experience, it was just a matter of me believing in myself. My belief came from the inside and it radiated outwardly. Others saw the belief I had in myself. Everything starts from within in order to materialize outward. Believe in yourself conveniences others to believe in you. If I did not believe in myself I would have never gotten to the point to put myself in the position to receive the opportunity that he had given to me. It would have never been exposed to me. Belief in myself opened up doors, to get me into arenas of other opportunities.

"MAKE YOUR MARK HERE NOW BECAUSE YOU NEVER KNOW WHO YOU MAY INFLUENCE LATER."

-Lamont Troy Taylor, Sr.

At this point the owner is thinking that my credibility is good or how else would I already be there. Then I find myself giving him a quote to maintain his building. That was my first commercial cleaning contract. That contract was for $24K a year and that was only for Monday thru Thursday for a few hours a night per week. And it just began to snowball. Now I have the reference of a big company so I go to other companies who were in construction and I kept getting references and it just went from there and just snowballed. Then I decided that I wanted to get in good with the local realtors because I knew that they sold a lot of houses and had to get the move in and move out houses ready I started to give a lot of the marketing materials to them and I started to get a lot of work through their rental programs and their vacation rentals. I was surprised to find out that a lot of the vacation rentals were willing to paying me a $100 a house on Saturdays because most people rented them from weekend to weekend and I was doing about six of those on a Saturday.

At this point I had my wife helping me and a couple of friends that did not have anything else better to do. So then I started thinking man this is good money but it is only on a Saturday because vacation rentals only run

Saturday to Saturday and then I thought about apartment complexes because they have people that go in and out all of the time. So I continued on to distribute my trusty fliers. I was banging on the apartment complexes leaving my flyers behind and with my incredible business references they just automatically wanted to do business with me.

"IT'S OKAY TO TAKE ON MORE… JUST BE PREPARED TO MEET THE DEMAND."

-Lamont Troy Taylor, Sr.

Because of the other opportunities I just could not strike out or lose out it seemed. So then the money just started coming in and I started getting crazy. I just started thinking "I want to clean the world". I wanted to be the biggest janitorial business ever! I started going over to the Western Shore putting out information and I ended up purchasing a cleaning franchise on the Western Shore. Once I purchased a cleaning franchise over on the Western Shore, I started cleaning car dealerships, huge post construction cleanups and office buildings. Even with all of this success, cleaning just was not in my heart and the lack of passion for the business reflected.

Now I have buildings that I am cleaning and some of the buildings are so huge that I have to have walky-talkies in them to communicate with my employees. Some of the buildings were a quarter of a mile long. Some were located in Maryland, Delaware and on the Western Shore. The business, at this level of determination the cleaning business peaked within a six to twelve month span.

"IF YOU DESIRE IT, IT WILL NOT BE DENIED."
-Lamont Troy Taylor, Sr.

Now, if you are ready for some more and I do not know how to put this, but at this point, I still have no experience and I'm trying to learning as I go. I am at 25 buildings, I am doing residential cleaning, I have two offices, vacation rental cleaning, apartment complexes, post construction cleanup, and the only experience I have is the cleaning skills that I needed to clean my own home. As much experience as I had then is "its dirty... you clean it up". As time went on it started to show, quality control was starting to be apparent because of the size of the business and the quality control inside of a business. The only way I can explain it is if you go see one of the rodeos it was like a wild bull that you ride and it keeps bucking you and I started to lose control of it. I did not know how to say no when the phone rang. Everything was "yes I can" when the phone rang…"I will take it!" I kept placing ads in then newspapers and the yellow pages. I kept getting calls from huge companies that wanted to subcontract their work like huge fabric store and so forth. I think I pretty much hit my peak.

> ## "THERE IS NO BETTER FEELING THAN THE FEELING WHEN YOU PROVIDE FOR OTHERS."
>
> *-Lamont Troy Taylor, Sr.*

This cleaning business ended is 2006 and started in 2000. I lived well for those six years but I tell you I hear it all the time. You know even with making the money and everything I think I enjoyed just the freedom. I enjoyed being able to go in the store and not make a financial decision as to whether or not I could get it. I enjoyed being able to surprise my wife with gifts. The ability to give something to someone and have the joy of seeing them enjoying the gift. I loved the ability to see the happiness from giving. The ability to throw a party and have everything set. The freedom it gave me to do certain things. I loved to entertain. I love to show people a good time. I love to go out and dine with friends and family. I bought rental property. I had this thing about owning property after being around and cleaning though rentals. I brought a rental property and I still own it. At least I invested some of the money. I loved my vehicles. I had to get my vehicles. All of my children were in private school. I donated money, but mainly to my local church. I was very active in my local church. I spent a lot of time there at Waters United Methodist Church. It was my home church. I am a still a member, but I know longer attend.

"IF YOU WANT IT TO HAPPEN... THEN MAKE IT HAPPEN!"

-Lamont Troy Taylor, Sr.

During the process of having the janitorial business, I had achieved a height that I thought that I could never achieve that encouraged me to go back to school. I thought if I could do this, I could go back to get my GED. Then I enrolled in my general education course and I remember going over and I had to take an enrollment or placement test because the teacher wanted to know what areas I had to work on and stuff like that so I took a placement test. I remember her telling me after I took my placement test that had I sat for my GED I would have past the GED test. All I had to do was take the test I did not even have to sit for the classes. The next test was not for a month later, the classes were free they were refresher courses, so I just took them anyway. I sat for my GED course and passed it. Then I was like man that was easy. Now I have a high school diploma. Then I framed it and put it on the wall. Maybe I should go to college. Then I went trucking off to the local community college and that started that.

"WE MUST CONTINUOUSLY EVOLVE WITH THE TIMES. YOU MUST KEEP UP!"

-*Lamont Troy Taylor, Sr.*

Even when I had the janitorial business I always had a lure for technology and a passion for the internet and other technologies. Since the business I started self teaching myself web design because I had a passion for web design but I did not know how to do it. So I purchased some web development software and I just spent hours, literally ten to twelve hours a day just messing with the software and I became so familiar with it I began to learn how to use the software just by trial and error. I enjoyed it. I really did. I love that stuff. However, as time went on, I still had responsibilities; I still had bills and stuff like that. I ended up going back and getting a job. I ended up going back and becoming a counselor and working at a homeless shelter while trying to build my web development and hosting company. I got to help people. I got to counsel people and inspire people. I just had this philosophy that you just become successful or die trying. Either way you do not have anything to lose. If you don't try you are not going to become successful, so at least try. To this day people keep asking why I don't do the cleaning business because it took no effort for me to do it.

"IF YOU DON'T WANT MORE, YOU WILL NOT RECEIVE MORE"

-Lamont Troy Taylor, Sr.

What you are looking at is the soul of a man who is inspired to be better and to be more and wants others to be more. If I can be more others can be more. Life is precious. It is a shame to waste it when you can be so much more and are so much more. This is motivational and inspirational. Certain people are destined for certain things. There are some people who question "what am I supposed to be doing" everyone is not cut out to own a janitorial business, become a web designer, or a lawyer. You have to figure out which path is yours. Ask yourself: What is my destiny? What am I supposed to be? The answers will come.

"A PERSON WHO CEASES TO EVOLVE...CEASES TO LIVE"

-Lamont Troy Taylor, Sr.

If a person refuses to educate himself, he is basically sentencing himself to a life of stagnation. There must be a quest for self education. I just believe that we have to constantly keep evolving ourselves. To stop looking for knowledge is to just stop growing. I just constantly challenge myself to learn more about anything not just things about my industry. I think that we should endeavor to be better-rounded. This is just my personal opinion. I want to be the type of guy that makes a million dollars. I want to be the type of guy that knows how to sit down and eat and know proper etiquette. I want to be the type of guy that has universal knowledge.

My maternal grandfather came here from Caroline County Virginia. He lived and worked on his parent's farm. He never went to school because his help was needed on the farm working with his father. So from the time he was able to work all he knew was hard work. He told me when he became a certain age, a young adult his father had come to him and said (and it was very typical for this to happen during this time and day) "it is time for you to go out and make your own family and have your own life." So he packed up his stuff and got on a train or whatever and searched for work. Eventually he landed in Oxford, Maryland and he said he came to a house that use to border up people and you would go there and pay for a meal and they would give you a place to stay. He once told me "I went out the next day and started looking for work in the town and would come back".

Note: a very important part that I left regarding his work ethic.

While my grandfather still lived in Virginia he said that he use to have a neighbor when he was living on the farm and that after he got done his chores for the day he noticed that his neighbor had all of this wood that needed to be chopped up behind his house. He said "I noticed the wood. I noticed that my neighbor must have been working somewhere else and he did not have time to chop up wood by himself." He did not ask him if he needed any help. He would wait until the guy would leave for work and would cut all his wood up and stack it up nicely and neatly and then sit back and watch the guy's expression. Whenever there was work that needed to be done that is what my grandfather jumped in to do.

He did not understand why some of the other grown men were sitting around and not working. He just could not understand it and eventually he landed a job at a local Boat Yard where he held a job there for 75 years. When he died they had a huge sign made for him in his memory. It makes me feel proud because when you think of an honorable and respected man everyone should want to be like him. I remember somebody telling me one time "What would you have people say at your funeral?" That is how you should live your life because of how you want to be remembered. Based on that, I have huge respect for the way my grandfather carried himself by being an honorable and respectable man to his family, his church family, and his employers. When he started out working at the Boat Yard he had a wage of $7 a week. They took a penny off for NRA I am not certain what that is, but I remember my grandmother saying that "he makes $7 a week and they take a penny out for NRA." After doing some research, I found out that this stands for – National Rifle Association.

"KNOWING YOUR PAST IS CRUCIAL FOR DETERMINING YOUR FUTURE."

-Lamont Troy Taylor, Sr.

You see I think differently than the way my grandmother, my grandfather, and my mother thought. I have a very different mindset. However, I respect my grandmother's and grandfather's discipline. They were able to accomplish their goals and what they wanted in life, which was their ability to save and maintain their household. I told my children about where my family came from and about a lot of the conditions that were not that easy to deal with during their time. However, with those difficulties they had to face, they still were able to set their pride and stuff aside and do what was best for their family.

I remember my grandfather telling me that he was on a job and he had left with the boss and the foreman and they were telling him what they wanted him to do and they went inside of a restaurant to have lunch and how he could not go into the segregated restaurant, but was still expected to stand outside while they had lunch and wait to walk and talk with them after they completed their lunch. It was the period and how things were done and a lot of things that my children do not have to experience and I let them know about the barriers of their time. I tell them that for the most part my experience with my grandparents was very positive. They were hardworking so they had all of their needs met. They never experienced any poverty because they always worked hard, saved, and maintained. Their needs were met.

Had my grandfather still lived, he probably would not have understood the magnitude of the company and what it all involved. He would have understood that I was in business for myself, but it may have been hard for him to wrap his mind around it. He would definitely have been proud of me. However, he would be just as proud of me working a 9 to 5 to take care of my family or if I were to make $20 million dollars. His main thing would be whether or not I was taking care of my family and whether or not I am living right.

My grandmother would understand the concept of the business a little better than my grandfather. I remember at one time she discussed with me her desire to have her own business. She loved to cook and wanted to own a restaurant. She would have understood the entrepreneurial concept, but again she would have been just as proud if I were maintaining my family, taking care of myself and doing the right thing. That was primarily her main focus.

My mother would definitely be proud of me because I am an extension of her just as I would be proud of my children. The more successful they are the more it strokes our egos as parents. We are proud of our children no matter what. I think my mom would be proud of anything I did as long as I was happy.

"DEVELOP YOUR PASSION AND YOU DEVELOP YOUR DRIVE."

-Lamont Troy Taylor, Sr.

Can one develop passion or is passion something that someone has? Develop your passion and you develop your drive. My passion has given me the drive to work for long periods at a time. I think I received some of the strong work ethic from my grandparents. My work ethic is strong and mainly when it comes to things I enjoy doing. My work ethic comes in with things I like to do like working with software and the Internet. I could work and focus on different websites and layout concepts for 12 hours at a time just getting up to go to the bathroom. I just do not get tired when it comes to that. I love to create a new project. It's like making a new creation. Another think I am passionate about is getting into the mind of the customer as to what they want and then creating it is almost like molding some clay and getting it to the right point as to where it is exactly like what is in someone's mind. I enjoy that.

My work ethic is really high. I just do not get tired of it for some reason. I cannot get enough of it. Although with all of the success of my cleaning business it was never my first passion. I always gravitated towards the technology and the internet business. I think that this is why I did not stay in the janitorial business. I encourage everyone to start a business, but to do to a business in an area that they are passionate about doing. If you are not passionate about your business or believe in your business it will be difficult to endure the toughness and the rough paths in the business. The money is just a byproduct or a bonus.

"KEEP IT SIMPLE...KEEP IT MOVING."

-Lamont Troy Taylor, Sr.

Keep in mind that when I was doing my janitorial business my mindset was really different. My mindset was just thinking like a worker. I still had the worker mentality because I was working for myself. I still had the mind of "get the job" and "go do the job". I really did not have the mindset of getting the job and watching the business grow. It was based on a pretty simple mentality. Get the job, do the job, get paid, spend time with my family, be active in my church, and doing all of what a person may see as an all around good pillar of the community. Now my mindset as I look back on it has changed because I want more.

I feel that I am capable of even more than what I accomplished. It is not that I was not satisfied, but I feel I can achieve the same success, but actually more because I love it. I was kind of forced into the janitorial business because my hours were cut and it developed out of the need to provide food and shelter for my family. Being a janitor is all I knew so I took what I knew and capitalized on it. It happened that it just worked really well for me.

> ### "AS LONG AS YOU ARE WORKING TOWARDS YOUR GOALS YOU WILL GET CLOSER TO THEM."
>
> -*Lamont Troy Taylor, Sr.*

As long as you are putting one foot in front of the other you will always be moving forward. You do not always need hunger to follow a business idea through. I am still using some of the principles from the janitorial business. I still use the principles as far as getting out talking to people, letting people know about the services I offer. Whether I am out physically or on-line just letting people know that I am there. I am not as hungry now. I have passion. I did not have the passion before, but I was hungry, but I should be hungry now. I am not really hungry as much because I know how things will build. Before I was hungry I had no clue of waiting to think about what I should do. I was out there banging the pavements and getting the jobs. Now I understand the work will come if you handle the business and get things done, so I already anticipate that. I am not as hungry to grab the work and get it to come in. Back then I was certain if I stopped pounding the pavements if the work would still come in to my business. To date, I have been working with the computer business since 1998 because I started with the internet then. That is when I first started dabbling into the business and nothing has changed since then. The same passion is still there and I am still doing it. With different levels of success nevertheless but I never let it go. I did not get too proud for the cleaning business. I did not mind cleaning as a business the money was right. If the money is right, your pride will not get in the way.

> "AS LONG AS YOU UNDERSTAND YOUR IDEAS, IT DOESN'T MATTER IF OTHERS DO NOT."
>
> -*Lamont Troy Taylor, Sr.*

What really happened is that I noticed a lot of failures that took place in the past that I saw as failures and I have been able to end up using them as a growing experience. I think that my children would say about me that their dad is very intelligent and that he wants the best for us, but I would have to say that they do not completely understand me. I do not even know if it is possible at their age or any age because I am very complex to some degree and I have my own way of thinking but that is what makes me an individual and makes me who I am. That is what makes me unique. I embrace myself. Sure I would have done things differently but because of my quest for knowledge everything is a learning experience. I am learning every day I am constantly learning from my mistakes, my failures. In some way I am able to always go back and re-use it because I believe at the end of the day people have to live their lives for themselves. At the end of the day I believe that, that is what matters.

Doing things that it takes to be a winner is crucial. We need to reprogram our habits to take on a winning disposition in life. May it be our diet, our exercising, meditation or our relationships? We have to have positive relationships. The majority of people in America have poor diets because their eating habits have been retained from their parents and grandparents. When we shop we buy our foods based on our financial status as opposed to what is good for us. Purchasing things regardless of whether or not it is high in sodium and it is bad for us down the road. We must eat well for preventative measures. All of this is very important in all aspects of our life because we cannot conduct business properly if we are not feeling good. We cannot feel good if we are not protecting our bodies. I also equate our physical bodies to our measure of success. Most people who are not physically fit are because of lack of discipline. If you are not disciplined with your body, you may be less likely to be mentally disciplined with your business.

"MAKE THE RULES, FOLLOW THE RULES, AND LIVE BY THE RULES."

-Lamont Troy Taylor, Sr.

Rules are important because they create structure and if we don't have any structure you really don't have any guidance. We need to create rules in our daily life to have structure. Our days need to be structured so that we know exactly what we are doing from day to day we do not want to get up and not know what we are doing. This is why rules and structure are important. I live by a set of rules. I know exactly what I am going to be doing when I am going to bed and I know exactly what I am going to be doing the next day so that I get the most productivity out of my day. If you don't have that in place it is almost being like a piece of paper being blown down the street. You can blow either way because you are going around aimlessly.

So you should look at the next 40 rules and see how you can implement them in your daily life so you can see how they can structure your day by going by these 40 rules. It should increase your productivity so you can get the most out of your day. Your time is your invaluable talent and you cannot get it back. One does not know how much time they have so why waste it? It may sometimes seem kind of predictable but it is imperative when building a business. Because if you don't obtain certain goals or reach certain limits when it comes to building or growing your business it is highly unlikely that you are not going to reach them if you do not set them and this takes preparation. That is why people have business plans. The business plan in itself is a structured set of rules. It is a road map as to what a person wants to do with their company and the position it wants to take. A person has to be able to follow it in order to get there. That all falls with the same with having discipline. Discipline is a must because to follow the rules you have to discipline yourself in order to see your goals and to follow your rules through. Most of your unsuccessful people fail to discipline themselves. My opinion is that it all goes back to being a learned behavior that is taught to us by our parents because these are the first people who discipline us and tell us our first rules and first discipline. Discipline is a learned behavior and can become a form of habit whether it is a disciplined habit or undisciplined habit. For those who have little discipline you may need to recognize that you are undisciplined and then you need to structure yourself so that you can have discipline. This is where the rules come in because it is like a guideline or roadmap into getting your first set of rules. Even if you are a person who is undisciplined you can still become successful in gaining discipline. These rules that I am writing down I only know because I experienced them and then I found that they are necessary for becoming a successful entrepreneur. If I had these rules ahead of time it would have saved me a lot of time and a lot of costly mistakes that it took me into getting on the right path.

Lamont's 40 Rules to Raw Business Success

Rule Number One
Raw Hunger

Once you get that hunger, I found that for some strange reason you begin to become a magnet to like-minded people. I have yet to see it fail. If you have the hunger and the passion you will draw people and yourself to like minded things. If you are not hungry do not expect your situation to change. You are most likely to end up where you are headed. If you do not change the direction in which you are going you are more than likely to get off course. You need to get hungry to make a change. If you are not hungry, you are not searching for anything to eat. Do not worry about money, do not worry about how you are going to do it, if you are going to be a success or not, you must try doing it. Just decide that you are going to do it!

Rule Number Two
Relationships

When I say relationship I am not referring to marriage. Not everyone is going to be married, but they may have a significant other. If the other person is not supporting you it can make it very difficult on the amount of energy you put into your business and it can affect your success. Imagine if you had more people around you that

thought like you and had the same hunger and passion towards business and achievement. You would go a long way. Basically surround yourself with people that are like minded like you.

Rule Number Three
Stay Focused

When you pontificate, what tends to happen is that you are thinking and coming up with theories. It's not fact, it's not truth. It is just theory. What happens is we can get distracted with many distractions throughout our day. Things such as an individual's theory on a particular situation, television, movies and media are all things that pertain to entertainment purposes. If not taken in moderation it can lead to distraction and take us out of focus. How often have you heard someone say "I cannot wait to go home and see that talk show?" Or the daily gossip and other people's business instead of focusing on what's going on in their lives.

Rule Number Four
Decide

Decide what you want to do. Think about what it is that you have a passion about. Think about what it is that drives you. Imagine hearing the eulogy of your own funeral and what you would want other people to say about you when they describe what you decided to do with your life. That's the whole purpose. Make the decision and act!

Rule Number Five
Raw Knowledge

After you decide, you have to go out and seek to educate yourself. You have to find information and research what you want to do. You have to become abreast with what we decide we are going to do. Know the industry, know the business, and obtain information in the particular field of interest. Definitely submerge yourself into making a commitment to learn about what it is you decided to do. Learn as much as you possibly can about what it is that you intend to do. Seeking RAW KNOWLEDGE is a continuous endeavor.

Rule Number Six
Spirituality

It is important to focus on your spirituality. It is a key. We need to connect with our spiritual higher power no matter your denomination or religion, if any. It allows you to rely on something bigger than yourself. It almost allows you to relieve yourself of some burdens. You can release the burdens. The Higher Power is backing you. Take time everyday and recognize our Higher Power whoever or whatever it maybe to you as an individual.

Rule Number Seven
Believe in Yourself

If you do not believe in yourself, who else is? If you do not believe you are capable of achieving your goals, your success, and your business what else is there? You will find that once you start to believe in yourself others will start believing in you.

Rule Number Eight
Remove the Obstructions

We want to identify the things that have been causing us to be unsuccessful in life and become aware of those things. Most of us are not even aware of the things that cause obstruction into our daily lives. Some of these obstructions can be found in rule number 3- stay focused. But we have to identify our own personal instructions that hinder us from carrying out our own goals and reaching in life. For example, this is sometimes not easy. It may require:

   a. Putting distance between friends who are not with the same mindset that you are trying to take on

   b. Having to socialize with people that you are not comfortable with those people that you are not use to socializing. However, you will need to put these obstructions to bed. You will need to get over these obstructions so that you can move forward.

Note: Obstructions will be different depending on each individual's situation.

Rule Number Nine
Give Back

It is very important to give back. I cannot stress the importance on that. I do not mean necessarily in a financial way, there are many ways to give back. With your time, advice, leadership, give back by just saying something nice to someone. For example, I remember my Great Aunt that lived across the street. One day I was helping her out at her house and she was standing over top of me while I was weeding. After I was done I asked her what she thought about the job and she told me "Lamont, you know what… you are one smart young man." Out of know where she made this statement. I believed it and I have never forgotten it. That is what I mean about giving back. You never know what positive influence you are making on someone at that particular time when you say something positive to somebody to put a smile on their face. You never know what reflection it will have on that person. She may have gone on and thought nothing of it, but here I am over 30 years later still remembering. Because of that, I have told my children and other children "You are smart young men." Or "You are smart young women."

Rule Number Ten
Hard Work

You have to put the work in. Nothing is going to fall into your lap. We must apply works to our goals and our business goals. If you are not willing to work for it you do not deserve it in my point of view. We find ourselves working hard for things that do not even benefit us but we are not willing to put forth the effort to work for something that will change our financial future. So if you are not willing to work hard, you might as well stay on the path that you are on because nothing is a free ride. Hard work pays off in the end.

Rule Number Eleven
Raw Dealings

Good Raw Dealings. If you are going to start your own business supplying a product or service, just do good old fashioned clean business. If you are going to say you're going to do it or can do it…then do it. Do not make promises that you cannot keep. Become a man or a woman of your word. Put yourself in the position of the client. This is the easiest way to calibrate your-self on how to deal with the client.

Rule Number Twelve
Raw Talent

Raw talent is not necessary. A lot of people say "they can do it, but that is just them. I am not cut out for it." That's just not true. A lot of people just see other people as having raw talent that they do not have and they credit that to the person's success and that is more than likely not the case. You do not have to have raw talent. You have to have raw dedication. The talent will come. Most talent is a learning process. It can most definitely be learned. The more you do it, the better you will become at it. That is what happened to me. The more I did it the better I got to be in front of people. The more I sold my business the better I got at selling it. It is a continuum experience.

Rule Number Eleven
Don't Quit

Everybody knows that if you quit, nothing can be achieved. Never give up on your dreams. I believe that your dreams are you. They make up who you are. If you are not following your dreams that are installed in you then you are living your life as a sub person. You are not really living who you are. Just follow your dreams. Do not quit. Do not give up on them. You do not want to look back on life and have any regrets and say "I should have done this" or "I should have done that." You only have one life and you want to make the best out of it. For example, if I had stopped it would have been a lot of things that I missed out on and now I am thankful that I did not quit and give up. The only way that you are going to get there is to keep on keeping on.

Rule Number Twelve
Health

You should not neglect your health. What good is it having a successful business and achieving your goals just to find out that you cannot enjoy it because of poor health issues? Anyone can come down with health issues, but you should try to live as healthy as you possibly can to reduce the chances of being stricken with self-induced health issues. Most health issues are psychosomatic. Self –induced in relation to poor eating and lack of exercise and checkups. If you love yourself then you will be willing to put forth the effort. When people love themselves it shows in their outer physical appearance, conditioning, and their grooming. These are all signs of people that care about themselves. They care about how they appear to the world.

Rule Number Thirteen
Look the Part

You have to look the part, if you are going to be in business. Depending on what business industry you are looking to go into, look the part. Look respectable and decent, be well groomed. If you are going to be out and conducting business you should be well groomed, and look like you already have a successful business. I was in the service industry and I wanted to look like a professional and successful service man. So I went out and purchased uniforms that reflected my industry.

Rule Number Fourteen
Act the Part

We need to act the part as well. Change your mind set. Start thinking and acting like the business owner of that particular business. You are no longer an employee. You have to act a certain way. Sometimes it requires you not to be friends or socialize with the people that work for you. Always remember that you are an extension of your business no matter where you are. Even if you are not at work you still are a reflection of your business, so you want to act in an upstanding manner, because people relate you to your business. Think about if you had a law firm and on a Saturday night you are drunk swinging from the chandeliers and a few clients are there. Don't you think that it would be highly unlikely, that people will go to you for business after they see the way you act in public? People relate your actions with your capabilities.

Rule Number Fifteen
Improve Your Speech

This is an important rule. A lot of people may not think so, but this is an important rule when going into business.

Your Speech- How you talk or hold a conversation matters because people tend to equate your capabilities with the way you come across in your speech. A lot of times you could be disregarded from the very beginning just based on improper speech. You may never get to sell a product or service that you have even if it could be useful to the potential client. Because of the negative way in which you came off with your speech or dialogue they immediately shut you off. Proper speech and enunciation is a key to success in dealing with business clients. Disregard all slang.

Rule Number Sixteen
Preparation

Preparation is important because we need to think about what we are doing and how well we will come across to the client. You might have to do a preparation or a trial run just to get a feel for how the client will perceive you. Find out how you are coming across to the client. Make sure you are prepared in all aspects of your business whether it maybe marketing your company to a perspective client or giving an estimate to a perspective client. When you tell people you are in business. Be in business you must be able and ready to conduct business.

Rule Number Seventeen
Quality Control

Quality Control makes sure that no matter what you do make sure that it is done with the highest quality. Make sure that it is the best quality that you can give. Check and re-check your quality and service. Make sure that the end user is receiving quality. Don't be afraid to ask the customer or the end users how they like the product or service you are offering. Always get feedback.

Rule Number Eighteen
Get Feedback

Feed back is the backbone of your business. It is imperative to stay in communication with your customers. You need to know what your customers are thinking of you. The only way to know is to have some form of feedback in place. Do a survey; offer a free gift for your clients to give feedback on your customer service or product. You must maintain open communication lines with your client.

Rule Number Nineteen
Embrace your Heritage

Not embracing your heritage can really be a problem. Instead of embracing my heritage not thinking that my heritage was entrepreneurial, I did not realize that my mother and grandmother were cleaning for other people, in a sense they were self-employed. I just did not look at it that way. So actually, I came from a long line of cleaners. That was there all the time; I just did not notice it. I came from a family with strong business principles. Embrace your heritage. This is what makes you unique. This is what makes you different from the competition.

Rule Number Twenty
Install Values into our Youngsters

Youngsters can do whatever they want. They are leaders of tomorrow. They are our next leaders. Install the values into our young ones and lead by example. That's important. We want to prepare the hands that are going to take over our business. More importantly prepare the hands that will take over our governments, our communities, and our planet. They represent the existence of humanity.

Rule Number Twenty-One
Make Time for Yourself

You have to have your "me time". Me-time is time that is actually all about you. You spend your time for others and making sure they have everything. You have to have time for yourself. Spend time alone. Go for a walk. Clear your mind. Do whatever it is you enjoy doing by yourself. It is imperative that you just have "me time" that you just designate to be alone.

Rule Number Twenty-Two
Raw Business Plan

You have to plan because most people wake up every day and they are moving about aimlessly. They have not planned out their day, their week, their month, or their year. You need to give yourself some form of direction. You need to develop a plan and stick to it. The key is to have some direction.

Rule Number Twenty-Three
Be Creative

Just because it has not been done before does not mean that it will not work. Be creative. Be on the forefront. Get creative in your marketing. Most of the times we tend to follow everyone else's lead in conducting business whether it is marketing or selling our products or services. We tend to mimic others that are already in the industry and less time on being creative.

Rule Number Twenty-Four
Stay Current

Staying current is a must because with the technology, the economy and the way things so drastically change now, we have to stay current on what is taking place in our industry in order to maintain a competitive edge.

Rule Number Twenty-Five
Understand your Money

Understand how to make your money work. Learn to invest back into your business. Become abreast with good money management principles. Understand how to make your money work for you and your business. Do not co-mingle business money and personal money.

Rule Number Twenty-Six
Use Your Time Wisely

Keep in mind that your time is your life and every moment that you waste of it you are actually wasting your life. Your time is also your money. So make wise choices on how you spend your time so that it may be beneficial to you. I would say that you should view your time as something very precious and not as something to be squandered away.

Rule Number Twenty-Seven
Think Ahead

Always think of the future of your business. Remember that you are not just in business for today. You are in business for tomorrow. Building your customer base is imperative to the success of your business. So you constantly want to think of your future customers. A percentage of your time of your workday should be dedicated to recruiting new business and maintaining support for current business.

Rule Number Twenty-Eight
Develop Tough Skin

You have to be able to accept rejection everything is not always going to be a "yes" or smooth sailing. You may from time to time have setbacks. But you must learn to develop a tough outer layer against those negative experiences that may arise.

Rule Number Twenty-Nine
Stay in Business Mode

What I mean by that is to be prepared to take advantage of every opportunity no matter where you are. If the opportunity arises for you to do business, be prepared. Always have business cards on you. Always be ready to share your product or service when appropriate. For example: You do not want to be at a funeral trying sell something. Always think of how your business can fit in.

Rule Number Thirty
Raw Behavior

When in doubt treat others the way you want to be treated. For example, if you were to purchase a product or service, what do you expect for your money? Place yourself in the role or the seat of the client. What would you expect if you were to purchase a product or service? You cannot go wrong with that. You deliver to people what you would want delivered to yourself.

Rule Number Thirty-One
Raw Mission Statement

Have a raw mission statement. This is important for the direction of your company. This is also important so others may know the direction of your company. Developing a raw mission statement is important to set the tone of your company's goals.

Rule Number Thirty-Two
Never Say "Can't"

Never say that you can't do something. There is no such thing as can't, only the people that will not apply themselves or see things through. Those that apply themselves say "I can". Those that do not apply themselves say "I can't."

Rule Number Thirty-Three
Have Confidence

Most wimps lack confidence. Have confidence. Stand tall. Believe in what you are doing. Project confidence in what you're doing. Nobody will follow a leader who is not confident in themselves. Most people look for people to lead them. So displaying confidence is an essential part of being a business owner.

Rule Number Thirty-Four
Take Chances

Do not be afraid to take chances. Nothing is guaranteed. Part of being an entrepreneur is to step out on your faith. We have to cut the strings of so called "security". The people that work the 9-5s are just entrepreneurs themselves. So take a chance!

Rule Number Thirty-Five
Reward your Achievements

Give yourself a pat on the back for your achievements. No matter how small or large they may be, they are all milestones in your business advancement, so recognize them and award your achievements. For example, treat yourself to that item that you had your eye for a while that you have always wanted. Go out and treat yourself to a nice dinner. Buy yourself a new outfit. Do or buy something that makes you feels good because that is your reward. It is all about rewarding yourself for your achievements. As an employee you receive bonuses and receive rewarding statements from time to time such as "keep up the good work" if you are doing a great job, but as a raw business owner there is no one there to do it for you, so you have to become your own reward person. This is a good practice because you will see the visual fruits of your labor.

Rule Number Thirty-Six
Have Passion

Have passion in what you do because this will definitely prove to be valuable through the slow times in business. Your passion will definitely sustain you. Imagine your business being successful. See it in your mind as doing the things that you want it to do. Maintain that passion.

Rule Number Thirty-Seven
You Must Set a Standard

Set a standard for your company. You must set a standard because this dictates the level of output of your business. As the owner of your company you must set the tone because everyone looks to you for direction and leadership, so you set the tone. You set the standard. Set your standards high.

Rule Number Thirty-Eight
Raw Positivity

This means remain positive. Always have a positive outlook. See things in a positive light. Try to not see things in a negative light. Even if something appears to be negative, look for the positive in it. We never see the positive in things. We always seem to see the negative. Maintain a raw positive attitude in everything that you do.

Rule Number Thirty Nine
Be Organized

Organization is important because you need to understand where you are going and what you are doing at all times. If you are unorganized in your business area, then your mind is unorganized. IF you are cluttered in business, your mind is probably cluttered. You must be organized. Have things organized. For example: Your schedules, your events, time you have to apply for business, time to apply for your personal life. You must have organization in your schedule so that these lifestyles will not conflict.

Rule Number Forty
The Raw Inner Feeling

The inner voice that is talking to you, listen to that inner voice inside of you. Follow your gut instincts if you feel good about something or pursuing something. Listen to that inner instinct. If you feel a little negative towards a particular thing or adventure, listen to your gut instinct. Try to develop your awareness of your inner instinct because it is there for a purpose. It is almost like a little built in homing beacon.

The previous Forty Raw Rules for Business Success have proven to be an intricate part of my business success and I feel that if you apply these same rules and principles they can be a great tool in your life and business. Don't just read them, submerge yourself into them. These principles are timeless. Let them become you. Read them, read them over and over and as often as necessary. After reading these rules, I still find myself learning new things. Rules are what they are. They are there for a reason. You can follow them or break them. It's your choice, but I suggest that you follow them if you intend to be the best and do the best that you can possibly do.

The forty rules are universal rules that can be used in your business or personal life. But now I'd like to share with you my 23 raw business policies. They are essential to the daily functions and growth of your business because you will need to develop some form of info-structure and my business policies go into step by step details describing how you can apply these policies in your current or start-up business. They include: The importance of not being sided-tracked; understanding your raw business location; developing your raw business image; presenting a positive business attitude; evaluating the necessity of a raw business vehicle; making sure you establish repeat business; staying grounded in your business philosophy; targeting raw niches; exploring the mind of your customer; always delivering high raw quality; executing quality control; knowing the market and where you stand; developing your ability to read your client's body language; recognizing business opportunities;

getting referrals; how to cope with pitfalls in your business; raw marketing tactics; never forgetting the customer is king; educating yourself as an ongoing process; maintaining your raw schedule; developing an understanding on how to push people in the direction that can be most useful; dedicating yourself to your business; and most importantly knowing the raw YOU!

Lamont's Raw Business Policies

LRBP No. 1
Don't Get Side-tracked

I think that it is very important not to be side tracked or focused with mundane things such as dating a whole bunch of people at once. Relationships with numerous boyfriends and girlfriends are just another way of getting caught up in trying to impress other people and these are distractions which can cause you to keep your eye off of both your goals and your rules for structure. Maintaining your focus is a key to accomplishing the things that you want to do in life. Note: this just does not apply in business matters only this also applies in all the areas of your life. So my advice to anyone who is trying to start a business, maintain your focus as to what you want to do and do not allow yourself to be sidetrack by surrounding interests. I am not saying that you have to be anti-fun. I am just saying that there is a time and a place for everything. So sometimes you may have to sacrifice having so called fun in order to get more important things accomplished. Work hard now and play later is what I always say "work hard now so that you can play later".

You do not want to be sidetracked with:

1. The Television

2. Comedies, Sitcoms, the stories

3. Sidetracked in gossip and talking about others behind their backs and trivial gossip. Stop being concerned with the business of others. Be concerned with what is going on in your life.

4. We should look at things from this point of view. How does it benefit me? And how is this productive? If it is not productive to bettering yourself or someone else then what is the purpose?

Think about how important it is for those of us that have children. They are the next generation and what you are learning here should be taught and installed in them so that they do not have to wait until they are older to read a book like this to get them back on track. A lot of these principles in this book are just good principles in life period! They can be used in helping to raise your children. Some can really be applied child rearing. Once you start thinking this way, it seems that you start to lure like-minded people around you because you start to seek out people that are thinking on the same level as you are. This is important to surround yourself with like-minded people. That is why I suggest that people should join:

1. Local Rotary

2. Local Chamber of Commerce

Joining groups like these are important because this helps entrepreneurs get around like minded people that are doing the same thing that they are doing. It will help bring forth opportunities for your business as well as serve as a good learning experience.

LRBP No. 2
Raw Business Location

I started off working at home. Now that I am thinking about it I did act a little prematurely when it came to setting up an office. Depending upon the business you are in I think that you should work as much as possible from home and cut your overhead. You should use your money to remarket and invest back into your own business. However, for some businesses offering professional services and security purposes, you may need your own off-site location. Sometimes at home is not a key place because that is where your distractions such as your TV, your radio, the refrigerator and depending on whom you are… children. People tend to be more professional when they are working out of an office than when they are working out of a home.

LRBP No. 3
Raw Business Image

Your business image is very important because it is how people perceive you. It is the first impression that people get of your business and it is from your business image, so you want to maintain a professional image and an image of quality. Just take a look around at other businesses where you go and spend your money and ask yourself when you establish your business image "Will I come and spend my money if someone else were doing this?" I use to test my image by engaging people in general conversation with people that did not know me and ask them about my company to get their unbiased feedback and whether or not they have heard of my company. I would ask them "what do you think about this company?" "Do they look like a good company?" And I would sit and listen to their responses and get an idea of how others perceived me.

LRBP No. 4
Raw Business Attitude

I really did not have much of a business attitude other than the fact that I was very hungry and wanted to be doing business. Again my attitude was a learned attitude. As time went on and I made mistakes and I saw what worked and didn't work my business attitude began to change because of my experiences. But for the starters all I had was a desire to be in business. That is all I had and that is all you will need. That's it!

LRBP No. 5
Raw Business Vehicle

Your business vehicle is important. However, it weighs a lot on what type of business that you do. Some businesses require that you pull up to the person's house, so again that goes back to your business image. How do you want your client to perceive your business when you pull up in their driveway to sell your business? In other businesses your client may never see your car so it may not be as important. But no matter what don't let that stop you. Work with what you have. At the end of the day just work with what you have until you can do better. Not having a raw business vehicle is not an excuse as to why you can't get started. Ultimately at the end of the day the customer is buying you. You sell your company. You are the living breathing entity of the business. You are the one who communicates. If the client likes you then the chances of selling your products or services are good. If you can establish a good rapport or relationship with your client they can get passed other things. That is because they get to know you. I know that from experience. For example, people who actually know you can see you when you are not in business mode and not be put off or concerned with the services that I can provide them and that is because I have developed a relationship with those people. That is why it is important with any customer before you try to get money from them or sell them a service to get to know them personally before you try to sell your service BECOME THEIR FRIEND FIRST. It is all about having a good relationship. When you have a good relationship you have clients for life. Others can come up to them with a cheaper price and they would refuse because they will hire a person they know have a history doing business with over an unknown person that they are unsure of whether or not they can deliver it at a lower price. However, I have to add that when meeting a new client, it is imperative that you put your best foot forward for everything from your appearance, your hygiene and your professionalism. The first judgment they are going to take is what they see before they know you. We do not want the potential client to put up any barriers based on their preconceived notions.

LRBP No. 6
Establishing Repeat Raw Business

Now you can go back to previous customers and sell them other services that you offer because at this time you have their ear. You have done what you said you were going to do. You delivered when you said you were going to deliver. You have shown them reliability and stability. When you go back to previous customers they are open to what you have to say, so you have to believe in what you are doing. Most successful business people believe in what they are doing. They are not in to make money. They really believe that they are helping people. That is the mindset that you want to have. It shows a genuine concern. It shows that your primary interest is in what you are doing instead of selling to make money. I have learned that I actually do better when I show the client that I am concerned and that the service that I am offering is helping them to do better. In short, the service is primarily to help and not just an exchange for money. That is the mindset of most successful people and it should be yours also. Really believe and act in a manner in which you are doing business solely to help the client. That is really important.

LRBP No. 7
You Must Always Maintain a Raw Philosophy

You must always maintain a philosophy of constant improvement. There is no plateau. You have to constantly be better and improve yourself because the completion is always improving. You will spawn competitors. People will look at you and say "I can do the same thing", so you have to constantly stay ahead of the competitors and constantly improve your service and research your industry.

LRBP No. 8
Find a Raw Niche

Find niches. Niches are very important for a couple of reasons:

1. It is a need for a product or service that very few people, if any are offering so it is a prime position for you locate your company in that area

2. You can look at niches from bigger companies. You can find a niche within a bigger company that is finding a product or service. For example: a social on-line network that everyone uses designing homepages for that on-line network would be a niche of a bigger company. A

lot of people may not know how to design home pages or have custom designs for that social network so that becomes a niche.

3. You have to look hard for niches. You have to have your eyes open and become aware of them.

LRBP No. 9
Get into the Mind of the Raw Customer

You must get into the mind of the customer because you need to understand what the client wants. Most people make the mistake of going to the client and they talk themselves out of a sale because they tell everyone what they sell and they have not listened to the customer or client first. Understand what they want and understand what they need first and then tailor it for their needs. You have to understand what the customer wants before you try to do anything. If you go running your mouth before you listen to client they will shut down. They may buy it, but they will feel remorse, not like it and you may not get repeat business. I listen to what my customers want and I understand what they want. This goes back to developing a relationship with the client at first. Becoming their friend understanding who they are and getting to know their personality. Once you understand that you will have a better understanding on how to fulfill that client's need whether it is a product or service. KNOW YOUR CUSTOMER.

LRBP No. 10
Raw Quality Control

When you have others that work for you once your business reaches that level you have to understand that the majority of the employees are just looking to get a paycheck, getting ends to meet or to just get the money and it is not a necessity. You will have to give them guidance and have a level of quality control in place to govern your products and services because at the end of the day your name is on the business and you will be held accountable. They will judge the quality of business based on the service that you or your employees render. It is imperative to train your employees properly. Have a mission statement. Train them to understand what your company offers and how your company offers it.

LRBP No. 11
Develop a Raw Relationship with Your Employees

It is important to develop a relationship with your employees because they need to have an understanding of you and the direction that you plan to take your company. You need to make sure that you are on the same page that they are on. When you are not around these individuals represent your company. In the essence they are an extension of you. You will need to have them properly trained. You will need to know their good points and bad points so you can place them strategically in different parts of your company. This is not difficult when you place ads for hiring. Nowadays people issue resumes and you can have an idea of where their experience lies and you can place them in positions that are needed. But the main key is to be upfront with them and be clear as to what you represent and what you expect of them. No beating around the bush and worrying about hurting their feelings. You have to be clear as to what they expect of you and what you expect of them.

LRBP No. 12
Raw Pricing and Servicing

Your company should be able to be duplicated. Someone else should able to follow your plan and run the business the way you run it. IF you do not have a plan people tend to shoot from the cuff. They may quote a price here and the next time they forget the quote because they do not have a standard guideline in place. That is why sometime businesses have the shooting from the hip in place. It is a sign of lack of experience. People who are in the industry should know what things are going to cost and understand pricing. When I was inexperienced, I quoted wrong prices. As I learned what a job would entail I got better at quoting prices. If you start your business at another location, your employees should be able to run it as efficiently as it was ran by you. Friends, relatives, and all others should get the same pricing. The business should run on a system. The same price you give a stranger should be the same price you quote a friend. You have to look at a business as its own entity. Prices should be set and have a set system.

LRBP No. 13
Be About Raw Business

When I had the cleaning business, I did a job for a woman who really liked my work. She referred me to one of her friends and I went out to give the lady an estimate and it took me roughly 50 minutes to get to the lady's house. She was that far out in the country on the water and just by looking at the house I could tell that she was affluent and I personally admired the house. I remember walking inside and I looked up at the ceiling and around at the walls and I gave her a compliment on the house. I said "This is really nice" her response was "ooh ooh…I guess you are going to sock it to me now!" So always remember that you must conduct yourself for business. If you are there for business, be there for business only. You must conduct yourself that way. It was my opinion that she had automatically assumed that because I saw her wealth she may have felt self-conscience about it and assumed I would over- charge her based on that. Once she said that I immediately knew where it was going and I had to reassure her by saying that I work in houses like that all the time, but that I liked the structure of hers and we got passed that milestone and we were able to conduct business. I learned to never do that again. Personal compliments can be taken the wrong way or out of proportion no matter how innocent it may be. If you are doing business ... be all about business... totally!

LRBP No. 14
Raw Referral

If you take care of the customer you can assure yourself repeat and referral business. Treat the customer like you want to be treated. You cannot get anymore raw or simpler than that.

LRBP No. 15
Marketing a Raw Business

Fliers work on the grass roots level. Fliers almost always work and do not be afraid to take those around. Knock on doors depending on what type of business you are offering. You may have to go through residential areas and knock on doors. It may become necessary to do that. Again networking with your local rotaries and chambers of commerce are highly recommended. Get creative on places you want to put on fliers. Get with the newspaper and do want ads. Get them on windows, doors, stores, and try to saturate areas as much as you can with your fliers.

LRBP No. 16
The Raw Customer is KING!

The raw customer is king. The customer has to always be the main focus. The main focus should always be the customer because even though we are self-employed we still work for the customers. Without the customer, there is no business, so the customer has to be the main focus. Pleasing and satisfying the customer has to be the first goal.

LRBP No. 17
Raw Education

Education cannot stop you; however, you must remain knowledgeable of your industry and try to educate yourself about your industry. Learn as much as you can. It is an ongoing process and it never stops.

LRBP No. 18
Raw Scheduling

Do not get too overwhelmed. Try not to do everything in one go. You have to plan and take steps and do everything you have to do instead of planning and getting overwhelmed.

LRBP No. 19
Raw Pusher

Go after what you want. A lot of people do not know there potential so you have to look inside your employees and give them an extra push. We have to at times be motivators. At times you have to motivate the customer. You may have to go back more than once. You just cannot drop off materials to a person once. You may have to go back several times and be persistent.

LRBP No. 20
Be a Raw Character Reader

It is important to be a raw character reader because you need to understand your client especially if you are talking to your client and trying to sell a particular service or product. You need to be aware of their body language and if you are holding their interest. This will help you build your service or product efficiently when thinking of the end user or client. If you are talking to a client and they are starring at the ceiling it is highly unlikely that you have their attention. You may need to change the subject, speak up louder to get their attention. You may want to call their name. Most of the time when you call people by their name you might just get their attention. You do not want to be overbearing and get threatening with your eyes because people like to equate that to your honesty. Watch for little frowns. They may not realize that they are doing it but because they are thinking about doing it is just a natural reaction. Pay attention to eye movement. It is also good when it comes to negotiation because it can help give you an upper hand. When negotiating it can help give you an idea of just where you stand with a client and these things can be important. For example, as I mentioned with my first customer in the janitorial business I knew because of the fact that I was pulling up in my own personal vehicle instead of a detailed logo service van with my company displayed on the side, because I had not made an appointment to meet with the client at their home, and because I had no prior experience or references, I knew that all of these things could work against me as far as the customer reading my character so I had to compensate by giving him a price that was so low that he would question himself as to not taking advantage of the opportunity that he was advantaged at the time.

LRBP No. 21
Recognize Raw Business Opportunities

Raw business opportunities surround us all of the time. We just have to tune in to see opportunities and I think the way to do that is to start taking on more of a business mindset. Start thinking about ways to make money and to see opportunities and once you get your mind fashioned in thinking this way you would see opportunities in things that most people just walk by everyday and never think of doing. For example, when I was riding down the street (maybe if you had seen me a year prior to that) a dirty house would have been a dirty house, but this particular time I was thinking about opportunities and it was presenting itself as an opportunity to make money and I acted on it.

LRBP No. 22
How to Handle Those Raw Pitfalls

Sometimes you have to handle the raw pitfalls. Life in business may often be subject to pitfalls from time to time. What I like to do is to be alone and to take a walk to gather my thoughts and to think about things other than my business. This is the time I use to think about how beautiful looking up at the sky and seeing how blue it is. Taking a breath in and feeling how good it feels. I notice the trees, the birds, I try to inhale that and take it all in. In some form or way I feel like I am connecting with it and it feels good. I just admire my surroundings especially being out in the country taking a walk. I also usually take that time to be thankful and to appreciate life because we all want to be successful in whatever we do, but me personally I like to back up from all of that and back up from it sometimes and appreciate life and what I consider my Higher Being has provided or established. I also search for enlightenment. This is when my mind is totally free of all the hustle and bustle of life. I think we should do that from time to time and step out of our daily routine. Be thankful for your children, if you are married be thankful for your wife and husband and the money you do have. If you think about it, there is always somebody less fortunate than you. Despite what little you have there is someone out there who has less, so I am thankful and it helps me to get through my pitfalls. You are not the only one going through pitfalls it is just that people are not talking about it.

LRBP No. 23
Knowing the Raw You

Get beyond your looks. After your looks there has to be substance there. Certainly we are visual, but get beyond what others can see. Ask yourself the following questions:

- "Who are you?"
- Do you know who you are?
- Do you need to give it some thought?
- What drives us?
- What are our motivations?
- What do we want out of it?
- What drives us?
- What type of person do we want to spend our life with?
- What do we expect out of life?
- What do we expect out of ourselves?
- What do we plan on doing?

One of my biggest things is we want to make a mark here. You don't want to come here to this earth and go out what I consider a molecule. Some come live and are just like a molecule. Then there are people who have done great things that changed history. They are recorded in history and they have left a legacy to go back. Those are the people who inspire me. They came and inspired people's lives. That is very important to me. Think about what you want to do in life and what you want to be and how you want to be remembered to make a positive change. Every day is the rest of your life. People are living and dying. Just like a particle in the dust storm floating. That may be okay for some people but to me I think that we are all more capable to do great if we set our minds to it and live to our full potential.

Making Good Financial Decisions

Now that you are energized to move forward and start your business or to ramp up current business, you need to learn to get in the habit of making good financial decisions with your money. Things such as keeping your business and personal money separated. First open up a business account. There are many ways you can go about doing this depending on how you want to get started. For those people who want to get started right away, you may want to decide to just become a sole-proprietor. This will allow you to open up your business account just by using your social security number. This will allow you to be able to deposit checks into your account using your "company trading as" name. This is the most inexpensive way to get you to be able to do business transactions and separating your personal and business accounts. Other ways are to incorporate. I am not going to give you legal advice, but you may need to seek professional advice from a certified accountant or a lawyer. However, you can incorporate as an LLC or INC and open up an account in your corporate name. The advantage here is that this protects your personal assets and it maybe better tax advantages. But the key here is separating your personal and business finances however you decide to do it. You must understand that you do not want to co-mingle the finances together.

Re-investing Back Into the Business

You will need to understand how to re-invest your money back into your business whether it is a product business or a service business. You may need to invest in your supplies or stock up on your inventory. Know that a percentage of your income must be dedicated to bringing in new business through marketing.

Keeping Some Liquid

You should always maintain a running balance because you never know when you will have to put your hands on your money for any situation that may arise. You can no longer act like you are living pay check to pay check.

It's Not Your Account...It's the Businesses' Account

The business becomes its own separate entity and it is not your personal piggy bank. You definitely should not see charges in your business account for the local video store.

Where the Raw Business Investment Comes From

The thing with the raw way is that you start getting money for the work that you do the services you do or the items you sale. So usually most people who start off raw start up with zip, you start building from that first sale. It is not the amount of that sale it is what you do with it. This is where the seriousness level of your business attitude comes into play. You can either take that money and spend it and then try to get another job and then spend it. Or you can re-invest that money and try to go out and get more jobs or sales. The Raw BUSINESS MAN OR WOMAN does not have the opportunity to go to the bank and get a loan. His or Her first source of investment funds is generated from his or her sales. So do not be discouraged if you do not have A1 credit, if you don't have any angel investors to invest in you or if you can't obtain a loan. Don't let these things discourage you. To give you an example and I certainly don't recommend it. Read the next section on A Raw Grass Roots Business Man.

A Raw Grass Roots Business Man

I saw a gentleman that was marketing his business outside of a local convenience store and he had business cards written in hand. It may not have been the most professional way to market his business however I left the convenience store knowing about his business and how to contact his business. He wanted to wash and wax cars. This does not necessarily require your name to be on a state of the art business card. He was a raw business man at its grass roots stage. The raw business man starts in his incipient stage and transforms into a more polished business man as he grows and re-invests. So never give yourself any reasons why you cannot get started TODAY!

See a Physician

We definitely need to pay attention to our health as a successful raw business man. If you are not healthy, it can cause distractions in the way you conduct business. Your full focus will not be able to be on your business because you may have to deal with health issues. Go have regular check-ups.

How to Obtain Coverage

If you don't have health insurance, seek your local government's community health plan, your local social service department or health department. You may eligible for something.

Preventative Maintenance

The most important aspect of your health is preventative maintenance. So we want to exercise regularly. Start off at your own pace. Especially if you have not exercised for a while, next is my disclaimer: Before performing any physical exercise, consult your physician to make sure you are capable to perform rigorous physical activities and exercise. In my experience as an athletically inclined person, I recommend anything that gets the blood pumping such as jumping jacks, push-ups, sit-ups, and walking. Ride a bike, swim, or do any type of exercising that you can do. You do not need equipment, treadmills, or to join a local gym. These things can be done right at home. Just do them! That is the key.

Offsetting Stress and Illnesses

In my opinion exercising MAY help offset stress and psychosomatic illnesses because it can get your oxygen and blood flowing. Get some time outside. Enjoy the outdoors. See the beauty in the sky. The environment is around you and the beauty in it. Look for the beauty in things that surround you.

Maintain a Balance

Other ways that you MAY be able to rid yourself of stress and stress related illnesses are by not overloading your schedule. Try to maintain a balance. Take some time for yourself. It is okay to be dedicated with your business, but you do not want to become obsessed with your business.

Your Intake is Your Fuel

Try to maintain healthy eating habits. Try eating foods with lower sodium. Eat fresh fruits and vegetables as opposed to junk food. Drink plenty of water instead of sodas. In my opinion by being selective of your fuel intake, it may prove to be essential to maintaining a healthy diet. Some studies show that eating healthier can increase your energy levels, strengthen your immunity system and even prolong your life. Your intake is your fuel, so what is driving your human vehicle?

Reach out to the World

In Closing, remember to always keep your business visible. In this day in time everyone who is anyone is on-line. Just about any business that is interested in high volume sales, a global outreach, and a desire to project a larger appearance will need be on-line. The first thing you want to do is:

a. Secure your domain name. This is the web address that people will use to find your business on the internet. Even if you are not ready to build your website, you need to secure your name because thousands of names are being secured daily throughout the world. The sooner you secure your name you can take it off the market. My company www.brutebully.com offers domain registration, hosting (a service you will need to display your website), logo design (this is necessary to create an image for your company), and also web design (designing your website to fit your product or service).

b. Keep in mind you want a company that can understand what you want to project to your clients or your customers. You want a company that is going to give you that personal relationship and work with you until you have a website that you feel will best represent your company.

c. Custom logo design is essential for branding your company that it may stand out from all of the other businesses that are in your field. www.brutebully.com offers high quality designs at affordable pricing. As a raw business person your funds will start low, but your global presence does not have to reflect it. Your raw business may start off with a small budget, but your identifying logo and website should not reflect that small budget.

d. Feel free to contact our office by email brutebully@gmail.com .

www.ingramcontent.com/pod-product-compliance
Lightning Source LLC
LaVergne TN
LVHW051702080426
835511LV00017B/2688